THE RETURN
OF PINOCCHIO

Richard Nelson

I0139945

BROADWAY PLAY PUBLISHING INC
www.broadwayplaypub.com
info@broadwayplaypub.com

Cover photo: Italy, 1945

First published by B P P I in *Plays By Richard Nelson, Early Plays Volume Two* in December 1998.
This edition: November 2017
I S B N: 978-0-88145-717-9

Book design: Marie Donovan
Page make-up: Adobe InDesign
Typeface: Palatino
Printed and bound in the U S A

THE RETURN OF PINOCCHIO was first presented in workshop at The Bay Area Playwrights Festival in the summer of 1982, directed by Richard Nelson and Robert Woodruff.

THE RETURN OF PINOCCHIO was produced by The Empty Space (M Burke Walker, Artistic Director) on 30 March 1983. The cast and creative contributors were:

PINOCCHIO .... Kurt Beattie
LUCIO .... Ruben Sierra
LUCIO'S WIFE .... Ruth McRee
LEONE .... Richard Riehle
MAMA .... Jayne Taini
SILIA .... Tina Marie Goff
ROSINA .... Suzy Hunt
CARLO .... Carlo Scaniuzzi
AMERICAN SOLDIER .... Reuben Renauldo Dumas

Director .... M Burke Walker
Set designer .... Scott Weldift
Costume designer .... Sheryl Collins
Lighting designer .... Michael Davidson
Sound designer .... Michael Holten

CHARACTERS & SETTING

PINOCCHIO, *a man in his thirties who once was a puppet who turned into a real boy.*
LUCIO
LUCIO'S WIFE
LEONE, *a newspaper editor*
MAMA, *his wife*
SILIA, *their daughter*
ROSINA
CARLO, *her son*
AMERICAN SOLDIER

The play takes place in 1946, first in a small village in Italy, later on a train in America.

NOTE

The title of each scene should be projected all the time
the scene is played and should remain in view for a
few moments after the scene is over.

for Seth Allen

Scene One
THE ARRIVAL

(Field near train tracks. Morning. A MAN *leans against a stick. He smokes. Train whistle in the distance—getting closer. He finishes the cigarette, with his fingers wets the end of the butt, then puts the butt into his mouth and chews. Train whistle closer. Suddenly a woman or girl's cry of pain is heard just offstage. He flinches but controls himself and continues to stare off. Train noise very near now and suddenly a man in his thirties falls onto the stage—he has just jumped off the train. He wears a U S O uniform. He is* PINOCCHIO.*)*

PINOCCHIO: *(To the train:)* Thank you, G I! *(To himself:)* I better make sure I didn't drop anything. *(Crawls around, then notices the man)* Hello.

*(*MAN *nods.)*

PINOCCHIO: Quite an entrance, huh? I jumped from that train. They wanted to stop for me—but orders are orders. But they slowed down.

MAN: Looked to me like they speeded up.

PINOCCHIO: Because they were coming down the hill. That's why they speeded up, but they speeded up less than they would have had they not slowed down so I could jump. That's what friends are for!

MAN: There are friends and then there are friends.

PINOCCHIO: Well, there aren't any better friends a man could have than my friends the G Is. What adventures

we've had together. We've been through thick and
thin. There's something real good about the Yanks,
never seen boys who love a good time better than
them. I'll give you a for-instance. I was on this train
going between New York and Chicago. And there
were these two G Is with me. Buddy, he was next to
me, and Speed was sort of kitty corner—there's always
somebody named Buddy or Speed in every crowd of
Americans. No matter where you go you can call out
those names and a Buddy or a Speed will answer and
befriend you and take you home and his mother will
make you soup and his sister who wears white socks
will laugh at your jokes—her boyfriend's name is Bret
and he's overseas, and the father, he slaps you on the
back and gives you whiskey to see how well you can
hold your liquor; anyway, there was this WAC who
was sitting there too, on the train, she's facing me and
all three of us guys, we'd been eyeing her, because
American boys always eye girls on trains though they
pretend to read books—mostly mysteries or books
about accounting, because all American G Is plan to
be accountants when the war is over—once they go
through night school on the G I Bill—so you see we're
looking at her and she has this run in her nylon; well—
Buddy, and we know this, he has a pair of nylons in
his suitcase—a brown suitcase with gold latches like
all Americans have—and he was saving them for his
girl, whose name is June and she's in California and
she knits sweaters for the Red Cross—now that's a
real American institution, the Red Cross, they have
chapters all around the world; but we watch this WAC
with the run and she notices us watching and we see
she's uncomfortable, and we know why, because you
see WAC's never have boyfriends so it's hard for them
to get nylons, so she's uncomfortable, ashamed almost
and you could even say sort of sad-looking. Well,
Buddy looks at Speed, and Speed at me and me at

Buddy, who now puts away his accounting book after
using a playing card with a naked woman's picture
on it as a bookmark, and after reaching up to get his
suitcase and unlatching it, he takes out the nylons and
puts his hand down in them. Well, Speed and I were
chewing our fists to keep from laughing; and then he
says to the WAC—her name is Heather, no I'm giving
too much away, forget that I told you her name—and
he says to her, I'm taking these home to my pa's farm,
he likes to use 'em as feedbags for the horses. And at
first she cringes, but then she laughs like American
girls laugh when they're being teased, American girls
just love to be teased, and we all laugh and then the
Negro porter comes by to say the dining car is now
open and then sort of shuffles away and later, in the
dining car, and imagine our surprise when we learn
that she's not a WAC at all but a WAVE and as WAVEs
are almost always girls whose fathers have money—
you see, that's why her name is Heather—she does
have a boyfriend, but, as he's Jewish, she doesn't know
if she'll marry him.

(Another cry of pain off)

PINOCCHIO: What's that? There's a woman over there?
What's she doing? Does she need help?

MAN: She's in control of the situation.

PINOCCHIO: She's with you then?

MAN: My wife.

PINOCCHIO: Oh. *(Short pause)* Well, I guess there's
nothing like coming home to get you talking about
your adventures.

MAN: Do I know you?

(For the first time the MAN turns to look at PINOCCHIO.)

PINOCCHIO: Lucio?! Lucio, is that you?!

(P<small>INOCCHIO</small> *tries to hug him,* L<small>UCIO</small> *pulls away.*)

P<small>INOCCHIO</small>: What's wrong? Aren't you happy to see me?

L<small>UCIO</small>: So you're back.

P<small>INOCCHIO</small>: Of course I'm back. I always come back, Lucio. Don't I always come back? Here, take an American cigarette.

(L<small>UCIO</small> *takes one.*)

P<small>INOCCHIO</small>: How is everyone? How's my Pa? Tell me everything that's happened.

L<small>UCIO</small>: There's nothing to tell.

P<small>INOCCHIO</small>: What are you talking about? You've lived through a war. You must have had some adventures.

(L<small>UCIO</small>'s W<small>IFE</small> *enters. She has a wire.*)

P<small>INOCCHIO</small>: Is this your wife, Lucio? Hey, not bad, Lucio. You know what they say in America?

L<small>UCIO</small>: *(To* W<small>IFE</small>:) Are you done?

W<small>IFE</small>: It's buried.

P<small>INOCCHIO</small>: What's buried?

W<small>IFE</small>: The kid.

P<small>INOCCHIO</small>: What kid?

W<small>IFE</small>: I gave myself an abortion.

P<small>INOCCHIO</small>: *(Reels back in shock)* Oh God! Why?

W<small>IFE</small>: We don't need more children. We have enough to do with the men.

(Pause)

P<small>INOCCHIO</small>: I see. I better get into town to see my father. We'll have a beer together, Lucio. *(Short pause)* I've brought American dollars with me. So we can have a beer together, Lucio.

(PINOCCHIO *leaves. Pause*)

LUCIO: You know who that is?

(WIFE *shakes her head.*)

LUCIO: His name's Pinocchio.

WIFE: Who's that?

LUCIO: His story's well known around here. His father was a cabinetmaker. One day he made a puppet and the puppet became alive. He was a naughty child and had many adventures, including once being swallowed by a great shark. Then a fairy turned him into a real boy, which was all he really wanted to be.

WIFE: What is this nonsense?!

LUCIO: No nonsense, it's true. He's very famous. Now he's come home from America. I thought I'd faint when I recognized him.

WIFE: Fairy tales!

LUCIO: Before the war such things were still possible. (*He starts to go.*)

WIFE: I gave myself an abortion and you give me miracles! (*She starts to throw the wire away.*)

LUCIO: Keep the wire, we may need it to fix something.

(LUCIO *and* WIFE *leave.*)

(*End of Scene One*)

Scene Two
THE ALPHABET

(*A small room—the town newspaper office.* LEONE, *the editor, sits at a table, setting type into a wooden galley.*)

LEONE: Damn. Where the hell is a "z"? (*Looks*) No, that's another "5". (*Puts it down*) Wait. (*Picks it up again and holds it to the light)* No "5". Mama, what did you do with my "z"s?!

MAMA: *(Off)* Check your pockets!

LEONE: My pockets? Why would I keep a "z" in my pocket? That woman has gone mad. I'm trying to typeset a newspaper, I can't find the letter I need, and my wife says to check my pockets. It's come to that. Life never prepared me for this. *(He checks his pockets.)* Nothing. Not even an "a", let alone a "z". Look what I'm doing. I'm taking orders from a crazy woman—is there no end to humiliation?

(Bell off. LEONE *doesn't notice it.)*

LEONE: I could just throw in a "q". Then it'd just look like a mistake—better that than having everyone think the town's newspaper is out of "z"s. I don't want to cause a panic.

*(*PINOCCHIO *has entered.)*

PINOCCHIO: Hello, Leone.

LEONE: *(Looks up, squints)* Who…? Oh my God! He's back! *(Jumps up, overturning the galley, letters fall to the floor)*

PINOCCHIO: Here, let me help you.

LEONE: I don't believe my eyes! *(He walks over the letters.)*

PINOCCHIO: Be careful, you'll break them.

LEONE: Who cares? I should have stepped on them years ago.

PINOCCHIO: Leone, sit down.

LEONE: *(Stomping on the wooden letters)* What good are they? You can't eat them. I know because I tried.

PINOCCHIO: Let's just get them out of the way. *(Tries to push them under the table)*

LEONE: I broke this tooth on a "c".

PINOCCHIO: *(Half under the table)* Leone, it's good to see you.

LEONE: The writing was on the wall. First the "z"s, then the "r"s would be the next to go until finally it's the vowels. That's death for a newspaper; take away a man's vowels and what's left for him to say?

MAMA: *(Entering)* I found a "z"; it was in your other pants' pocket. *(Sees* PINOCCHIO*)* Ah! He's back? *(She drops the letter block and runs out.)*

LEONE: She found a "z"! *(He dives after it.)* She could have broken it. See what she thinks about newspapers? You can imagine what I've had to put up with in my marriage.

PINOCCHIO: Where did she go?

LEONE: To get you something to eat, of course. Everything hasn't changed.

PINOCCHIO: She doesn't have to do that. I can buy food. I have American dollars.

LEONE: That's right. You're a movie actor now.

PINOCCHIO: I wouldn't say that. There was only one movie and I played myself. You could hardly call that acting.

LEONE: But you're famous.

PINOCCHIO: Even in America, the story of a puppet who turns into a real boy is unique enough to cause some celebrity.

LEONE: And you got paid.

PINOCCHIO: I'd be embarrassed to say how much.

LEONE: So be embarrassed.

PINOCCHIO: Though I've tried also to pay back, in the best way I could, all that I was so fortunate enough to receive.

LEONE: You gave the dollars back?

PINOCCHIO: No. Americans don't give money back. What they do, you see, is use their money or their time to in some way help their fellow Americans, those who because of bad luck have not achieved the success which they themselves enjoy. See, America is like a giant kettle where all the races and nationalities of the world have come together to live in peace, and after a year or so when they are rich, they use their fortunes to build hospitals with their names on them, or great universities with ivy and their names on them, or they organize picnics for orphans—orphans being the least lucky Americans, that is until they grow up and can make their own luck. And me, being swept up in this American way, I joined the U S O and have been entertaining the G Is in Europe. It's what we in the movies do to give back a little something to America.

LEONE: So you kept the dollars.

PINOCCHIO: Of course. Leone, let me look at you. I can't tell you how many times I've thought of you, here in this shop, each week putting out your paper. How could I ever forget, when it was you, Leone, who first wrote about me and my adventures in your little paper.

LEONE: They were more than adventures, my boy. They were miracles! The kind that used to happen around here all the time. I'll tell you something— the fun went out of running a newspaper when the miracles stopped happening.

PINOCCHIO: But Leone, they're still happening. Every day of every week in a place called Hollywood, U S A. Oh, I know you've heard stories about pushy

Americans groveling after every buck they can fit into
their fat wallets...

LEONE: I've heard nothing. Tell me.

PINOCCHIO: And that gruff exterior is certainly a part
of the American character, but before you criticize their
ways....

LEONE: Who's criticizing?

PINOCCHIO: You must first look at what these tough
Americans have accomplished, Leone. If you could
only see with your own eyes Hollywood, you'd know
to what purpose all this effort all this hard work has
been exerted. Hollywood U S A—palm trees like in
pictures, sunsets like in paintings, wide boulevards
over which rumble cars the size of boxcars; the
dramatic sweep of searchlights...

LEONE: We've had searchlights.

PINOCCHIO: The sky is blue, the grass green where once
there was only brown desert; and the homes, Leone,
and everyone owns at least one home, they are like
palaces for kings, which is what Americans are, every
man is his own king; and churches—Americans are
very religious—each bigger than the next. Exotic fruits
fall into your hands from trees which shade you from
the sun....

(SILIA, LEONE's *daughter has entered. She is pregnant.*)

SILIA: Hello.

PINOCCHIO: Who's this? Don't tell me you're little Silia?

LEONE: When you go away, Pinocchio, people grow
up.

PINOCCHIO: And get married as I can see.

SILIA: No.

PINOCCHIO: Oh. I see.

LEONE: It was either an American Negro sergeant. Or a lieutenant from Bavaria, or—who was the third possibility?

SILIA: A Sicilian laborer who had some stolen pork.

LEONE: You think it really could have been him? Those Sicilians are so greasy he probably slipped out.

PINOCCHIO: I think I better go.

LEONE: So soon? You just got here.

PINOCCHIO: I only came by to ask if you'd seen my father. I went to his shop but it was boarded up.

(SILIA *looks at* LEONE. *Pause.* MAMA *enters with food.*)

LEONE: Now you have to stay and eat or you'll hurt her feelings.

PINOCCHIO: Only a minute. But what were you going to say about my father?

(PINOCCHIO *sits.* MAMA *places food in front of him, and stares at him.*)

PINOCCHIO: Why is she staring?

LEONE: She's waiting for you to taste it.

(PINOCCHIO *tastes the food.*)

MAMA: That'll be one American dollar for the food.

(PINOCCHIO *looks up.*)

LEONE: And throw in two dollars more for damaging my type.

(*End of Scene Two*)

Scene Three
CARROTS

(A street. ROSINA, a woman in her forties, pushes an almost empty vegetable cart. She stops the cart, pulls out a rag and wipes carrots. She has only two bunches. Afternoon)

(PINOCCHIO enters. Looks at her. Pause)

PINOCCHIO: Hello.

ROSINA: Want to buy a carrot?

PINOCCHIO: It's me. Remember?

ROSINA: I don't need glasses. I have eyes.

PINOCCHIO: I'd thought you'd be surprised.

ROSINA: Word travels fast. You've been to Leone's.

PINOCCHIO: I guess I've forgotten what a small town this is.

ROSINA: Look behind you.

PINOCCHIO: *(Turns and looks toward the audience)* I know. Why do they keep following me? I've tried to find out, but the moment I start to get close they run away.

ROSINA: They're curious, to say nothing about hungry. Or maybe hungry, to say nothing about curious. You're famous.

PINOCCHIO: But this is my home. I grew up here. I couldn't be all that strange. They look at me like I'm from the stars.

ROSINA: Carrot?

(PINOCCHIO takes one.)

ROSINA: Ten American cents.

(PINOCCHIO pays ROSINA; eats the carrot.)

ROSINA: When the Americans came in here, somehow it got out that here was the village of Pinocchio. I suspect it was Leone. The only smart thing he's ever done. How many letters did he lose today?

PINOCCHIO: He's always losing letters?

ROSINA: Hasn't published a paper in three years. He's always missing a letter. He never got into trouble.

PINOCCHIO: And my father, Rosina, what's happened to him?

ROSINA: *(After a pause)* We had no idea how famous you were. We hadn't heard about your American movie career. But when they all started clicking their cameras we started to understand. Every G I wanted a snapshot of the village of Pinocchio. Until then, we had no idea.

PINOCCHIO: Americans and their cameras! I know just what you mean. But what about my father, Rosina?

ROSINA: *(After a pause)* One of the G Is, a corporal, he wanted to fix up your father's shop and charge the other G Is to take pictures in there—of course it was my brother's barn that he fixed up in the end, because it was more in the middle of the village, but when he was done it almost looked like Geppetto's shop, and he paid us to make puppets which he sold both here and shipped back to America. That was the best month of the war.

PINOCCHIO: There's nothing like American enterprise to make you see all that's possible. And that's a side of the American character that gets so much criticism. I for one just don't understand it.

(ROSINA *starts to push the cart away.*)

PINOCCHIO: Where are you going?

ROSINA: To earn a filthy penny.

PINOCCHIO: But what about my father, I'd hoped you would know where he is. You were, after all, his housekeeper.

ROSINA: *(After a pause)* I'd take you to him, but I have these carrots to sell.

PINOCCHIO: Here. *(Takes out money)* I'll buy them all. Now let's go.

ROSINA: You're going to eat all those carrots?

PINOCCHIO: No. I don't think so.

ROSINA: Then what are you going to do with them?

PINOCCHIO: Here. You can keep them. *(Gives her back the carrots)* Which way?

ROSINA: Later. I have these carrots to sell.

PINOCCHIO: *(After a pause)* Here. *(Takes out more money)* I'll buy them again. Now can we go?

ROSINA: *(Hands him the carrots)* What are you going to do with them?

PINOCCHIO: I'll eat them.

ROSINA: You can stuff your face with those hungry people watching you? *(She points toward the audience.)*

PINOCCHIO: Then I'll give them away.

ROSINA: You don't have enough for everybody. How are you going to decide who gets a carrot and who doesn't?

PINOCCHIO: *(After a pause, he suddenly throws the carrots into the audience.)* There!

(Sound of crowd fighting)

PINOCCHIO: *(Yells:)* Now take me to my father!

ROSINA: I'll have my son take you.

PINOCCHIO: Carlo?

ROSINA: You think I can afford more than one son?

PINOCCHIO: Why don't you take me?

ROSINA: *(Counting her money)* I want to go buy some cigarettes.

PINOCCHIO: *(Hands her some cigarettes)* Here. American.

ROSINA: Now I want to sell some cigarettes. American.

(Crowd continues to fight.)

(End of Scene Three)

Scene Four
AMERICAN CIGARETTES

(A cemetery. Wind. A single white cross. PINOCCHIO and CARLO [early twenties] stand. PINOCCHIO stares at the cross.)

(Pause)

CARLO: If you want to be alone.

PINOCCHIO: No. Stay. Please. *(Short pause, then he reaches into his pocket and pulls out a pack of cigarettes; he throws them toward CARLO without looking at him.)*

(Pause)

(CARLO looks at the cigarettes and then at PINOCCHIO. After a while he begrudgingly picks them up.)

(PINOCCHIO kneels before the grave and says a prayer in Latin. He crosses himself.)

PINOCCHIO: *(Without looking at CARLO)* It's a nice spot. Who dug the grave?

CARLO: I did.

(Pause)

PINOCCHIO: Thank you. *(Short pause, then he reaches into his pocket and takes out another pack of cigarettes. He turns to* CARLO.*)* I appreciate it.

(Throws the pack to CARLO *who again hesitates and almost with hostility picks up the pack.)*

PINOCCHIO: Does anyone know how it happened?

CARLO: *(Shakes his head)* He was dumped out of a car. One minute he's in his shop and the next he's being dumped out of a car. He wasn't tortured. It was quick. One bullet.

PINOCCHIO: What did he do?

CARLO: He sold food. And he sold his food cheaper than others sold their food. So they informed on him.

PINOCCHIO: Someone from this village?

*(*CARLO *nods.)*

PINOCCHIO: One of his friends?

CARLO: We were all his friends.

PINOCCHIO: It's hard to understand. But I guess we have to try, don't we? Look at the Americans. They've never been invaded. Not one of them has seen their cities destroyed, seen the effects of war on their day-to-day life. *(Short pause)* And yet, damn it, they know that. They know how privileged or lucky they've been and they know how unfair it is to judge, to point that accusing finger at others who have been living in a hell that they themselves have never known. My father murdered by one of his own friends; but what right do I have to criticize—how do I know how I'd react in the same situation? It's hard, but you must just try to be fair, to understand, like the Americans do. What a fascinating people they are; aren't they always the first to help, to roll up their sleeves and plunge in with all the help they can give. Lost, they'll take you into their homes, a fire burning, soup on the table, feather quilt on the brass bed, a hot bath in a polished white ceramic tub; hungry, they will feed you, meat and potatoes and pumpkin pie; sick, they will nurse you, dabbing cool wet cloths across your hot forehead and when you wake up there's the mother of the house, a gentle smile on her face, her hair in a bun, her apron folded in her lap. Thank God I have been there and I have learned so much. *(He gets up.)* Carlo, I want to arrange for someone to distribute the boxes of clothes and canned foods I'll be sending back here. With a little food in their stomachs and clothes to be proud of instead of rags, who knows how much of this would have happened.

CARLO: Then you're going back?

PINOCCHIO: Tomorrow. I found who I was looking for. *(Short pause)* Carlo?

CARLO: Yes?

(Short pause)

PINOCCHIO: The miracles, is it true, they've all stopped happening?

CARLO: It is true.

PINOCCHIO: No more blood of Saint Catherine in the village fountain? No wandering monks who change into ravens? No blind men to raise the dead? No talking birds? No flying fish?

CARLO: Nothing. Since the war.

PINOCCHIO: And that seems like a million years ago. No wonder everybody stares at me. I'm the last miracle they have. *(Starts to go. Stops. Turns back to the cross)* Damn it. He watched how I turned into a real boy, if only he could have seen how I've turned into a real man.

CARLO: Pinocchio?

PINOCCHIO: What is it? Oh right. *(He reaches for another pack of cigarettes)* Thank you. *(Gives them to him)*

CARLO: Pinocchio, there's something I should warn you about.

(PINOCCHIO turns back.)

CARLO: I heard my mother talking with some of her friends. The dollars you have, they were talking about how they were going to steal them from you.

PINOCCHIO: My dollars? How?

CARLO: During the night, they'll come to when you're sleeping. And the fattest, I heard, will sit on you; and the strongest, I heard this too, will cover your mouth so you can't scream, and my mother, who is the quickest, will take the dollars.

PINOCCHIO: Like the blind cat and the crippled fox.

CARLO: Who?

PINOCCHIO: They're an adventure from my youth— when thieves were cats and foxes instead of old women making a living on the black market. Where can I hide until morning?

CARLO: No where. Everybody's watching you.

PINOCCHIO: Then my dollars. I'll hide my dollars. You must know a good hiding place.

CARLO: I have a secret place where I keep some of my things.

PINOCCHIO: Take me there.

CARLO: It's secret.

PINOCCHIO: Then here, you hide the dollars for tonight, and bring them to me in the morning. *(Starts to give him the money)*

CARLO: Are you sure you trust me?

PINOCCHIO: I trust you.

(PINOCCHIO *turns away, quickly turns back, hands* CARLO *another pack of cigarettes.*)

PINOCCHIO: I trust you. *(He goes.)*

(End of Scene Four)

Scene Five
SIZZLING STEAKS

(Cafe. Table. Two chairs. Coat rack. Almost dawn)

*(*PINOCCHIO *with a bottle and glass in front of him. He is drunk.)*

PINOCCHIO: Set 'em up! One more! One more for the road! *(Points in a direction. Short pause, then points in another direction, as if he were figuring out which was the right road)* For the road! *(He reaches for the bottle, knocks it over, but catches it just in time, smiles about how quick he was. Then without looking he pours the bottle onto the table, missing his glass. Drinks from the glass. Wipes his mouth.)* Ah! Getting sort of warm in here. *(Loosens his tie. Struggles to take off his jacket, finally does and goes to the coat rack to hang it up. He misses. Bumps into the rack)* Excuse me. My fault. *(Hangs coat up, but the rack falls on him)* Fresh! *(Sets the rack back up, starts to move, stops, takes off his hat, looks around where to put it, notices one of the arms of the rack, sets his hat on it)* Thank you. *(Reaches into his pocket for a tip, tries to hand the rack a coin, lets it drop)* There's more where that came from, cutie. *(Walks back to the table; referring to the rack:)* Nice tits.

(Almost falls, recovers; SILIA *has watched the end of this; she has entered with another bottle. He now notices the bottle is empty.)*

PINOCCHIO: One more! And another one for the skinny
girl there. *(Points to the coat rack. Pause.)* I said one
more. Jesus H Christ, who's a fella got to fuck to get a
drink around here?

SILIA: Are you sure you haven't had enough?

PINOCCHIO: Who are you talking to? Someone around
here giving you trouble? Who's the loud mouth who's
giving this lady trouble? Just have me talk to him.

SILIA: It's nearly dawn. You don't want to sleep?

PINOCCHIO: Sleep? So you can do what? Gotch you!
Gotch you! Ha-ha. You fucking wops. You fucking
dago wops. You fucking dago wops wait `til he goes
to sleep and roll him thieves. See. Gotch you. Ha-ha.
What do you think, that I'm made of money? You want
a handout, then stick out your hand! Here. *(Reaches into
his pocket, throws some coins on the ground)* Leave that for
the cleaning lady. Or bring along all your barefoot little
dagos—that is, if they can take a break from sticking
their hands into other people's back pockets, or from
selling themselves to fat old men to play with. Wait—
no—that's the Greeks, not you dagos. Excuse me.
Even a man who works for a living makes a mistake
now and then. And I've made every red cent I have.
Nobody's given me nothing. I don't walk around with
my head down living in buildings that's all rubble.
I take pride in my surroundings. You got weeds
growing everywhere. You see what I'm saying? Am I
getting through inside your head? You little weasels I
never know what you're thinking. You walk so slow
it's like you don't want to get anywhere; you spend
half your life slapping mackerels, well what the hell do
you wops pray for anyway—for some fat American to
bail you out? Well, we'll do it once, but by golly you're
on your own after that. Well, we'll just pick up our
technology and leave you to pinch each other's ass in

the beautiful Mediterranean sun! We don't need you—
you need us! And the sooner you understand that,
the better it'll be for you! I'm tired of taking your shit,
what I want is a goddamn thank you. *(He goes to get his
coat)*

SILIA: You leaving, Pinocchio?

PINOCCHIO: I'm going back to where a man can sleep
under the stars, have a saddle for a pillow and keep
his gun at his side. And if any rustler or fox or Italian
woman wants to sneak up on him, let them try, 'cause
they're gonna get a bullet through the face. And I'm
not talking cities now, they're just the same shitholes
as this dago swamp—I don't want any Negro making
eyes at my wife; or if he does I hope to God I'm there.
(Short pause) No, I'm going where things are open and
there's nobody trying to climb on my back, where the
only weight you got to carry is your own. And your
families. I'm going where for dinner you cut off a nice
two-inch steak and you sizzle it on an open fire with
the smoke and smell swirling in the moon light. You
ever have a two-inch sizzling steak? *(No response)* I'm
talking to you. Have you? I'm asking, have you?! How
the hell can you call yourself a human being when you
haven't had a two-inch sizzling steak?!! I don't know
what's wrong with you people. *(He sits.)* You make me
ashamed. I'm so ashamed. *(He passes out.)*

(Pause)

*(SILIA looks at PINOCCHIO, then at the coat rack. She goes
to the jacket and checks all the pockets—she finds a few coins
and takes them. She turns to go, stops, goes back to the jacket
and takes it and puts it over his shoulders like a blanket. She
pats it. And leaves)*

(End of Scene Five)

Scene Six
FOOD

(ROSINA *beside her cart. Morning. She smokes.*)

(CARLO *enters.*)

ROSINA: Where have you been?

CARLO: On the hill watching the new Americans arrive.
Did you know they were coming?

ROSINA: Lucietta told me.

CARLO: Aren't you interested?

ROSINA: I was when Lucietta told me. Do I have to
be interested when you tell me too? Besides, we've
nothing left to sell. And what good are Americans
when you've nothing left to sell?

CARLO: I saw them unload the trucks. There must have
been a mile of them. One... (*He stops, looks off.*) Sh-sh.
(*He ducks behind the cart.*)

(PINOCCHIO *enters.*)

PINOCCHIO: Have you seen your son? He was
supposed to meet me this morning.

ROSINA: You think I can keep track of him?

PINOCCHIO: If he comes by, tell him I'm looking for
him. (*He hurries off.*)

CARLO: (*Standing up*) One—or at least one—was
packed in ice. When they opened the door, all these
chunks of ice fell out. That must be where they keep
the meat.

ROSINA: And the butter.

CARLO: And the butter.

ROSINA: Also the cheese.

CARLO: Do Americans eat cheese?

ROSINA: In little bits when they have their cocktails.

CARLO: Swiss?

ROSINA: No, American.

CARLO: Oh… And then they were unloading another truck and I saw them drop a crate. It smashed wide open. It was packed with cans.

ROSINA: Dented now.

CARLO: The cans?

ROSINA: I've been told Americans won't eat from dented cans.

CARLO: If they're hungry enough they would.

ROSINA: If they were hungry enough they would.

(MAMA *runs in, with a basket.*)

MAMA: The Americans are back, did you hear?

ROSINA: We heard.

CARLO: I saw them.

MAMA: Do you know how long they'll stay?

CARLO: They're putting up fences.

MAMA: Then they'll be here a month at least.

ROSINA: What's in the basket?

MAMA: I emptied out the barn. You never know what these Americans will buy.

ROSINA: You cleaned out your barn so many times, what could be left to sell?

MAMA: You never know.

CARLO: They've got trucks stuffed with meat. I saw the ice.

MAMA: Any fish?

ROSINA: You're getting picky?

MAMA: No. No. Meat's fine too.

CARLO: And American cheese, we think.

MAMA: What's that?

CARLO: It's not Swiss.

ROSINA: It's big. It comes only big, like everything American.

(CARLO *ducks again;* PINOCCHIO *enters.*)

PINOCCHIO: You still haven't seen him?

MAMA: Who?

PINOCCHIO: Carlo.

MAMA: What do you want him for?

PINOCCHIO: He was doing me an errand. We were supposed to meet up this morning before I leave.

MAMA: You're leaving?

PINOCCHIO: I have no reason to stay.

MAMA: Did you hear that the Americans have come back?

PINOCCHIO: Where?

MAMA: Over the hill. Thousands of them. And trucks too.

ROSINA: Crammed with meat.

MAMA: And maybe fish.

ROSINA: And maybe butter.

MAMA: I'm going to sell my last belongings to the Americans.

ROSINA: You won't get a penny for that junk.

MAMA: We'll see who's eating fish tonight.

PINOCCHIO: I'll go take a look on the hill. Maybe he's watching the Americans.

MAMA: Good idea. I'll bet that's just where he is.

PINOCCHIO: But if you see him…

ROSINA: We'll be sure to tell you.

(PINOCCHIO *goes off.*)

(CARLO *stands again.*)

MAMA: *(To* CARLO*)* What was that about?

CARLO: Who knows? He probably wants to say goodbye, give me a nice firm handshake, pat me on the back, and tell me to work hard and be good.

MAMA: Then I don't blame you for avoiding him.

ROSINA: Where's Leone?

MAMA: He's trying to start his truck.

ROSINA: He's going to sell it again?

MAMA: He'll keep selling it as long as he can keep stealing it back.

ROSINA: I wish I had a husband with a truck.

MAMA: The war's been especially cruel to you, Rosina.

ROSINA: Look—there's Lucietta.

MAMA: Oh, God. Where did she get that dress?

ROSINA: *(Calls)* Hello!

MAMA: Hello! Yes, we heard! Good luck!

ROSINA: She doesn't give up.

MAMA: Let her dream.

ROSINA: No American in his right mind would marry her. She hasn't a prayer.

MAMA: She'd take a crazy one.

ROSINA: Now your Silia is another story.

MAMA: She's been close twice.

ROSINA: I didn't know that.

MAMA: But in the end they only wanted a virgin.

ROSINA: Why a virgin?

MAMA: American men only marry virgins.

ROSINA: I didn't know that.

MAMA: That's because you don't have a daughter.

CARLO: When you two are finished let me know, because I want to tell you what else I heard.

ROSINA: What did you hear?

CARLO: I talked to one of the sentries and…

(LEONE *enters.*)

LEONE: I got the truck started. It should run a good thirty, maybe forty minutes before it falls apart again. Going to have to talk fast to sell it this time.

MAMA: Leone, Carlo's seen meat. And maybe fish.

CARLO: They have trucks packed with ice.

LEONE: You saw meat?

CARLO: I saw the ice.

LEONE: You think they have any mushrooms?

ROSINA: How can you think about mushrooms at a time like this when there's meat?

LEONE: When I think of meat I think also about mushrooms. Can't a man dream?

CARLO: They have cans—so maybe they have canned mushrooms.

LEONE: It'd be better if they were fresh. But I won't turn my nose up.

(CARLO *ducks again.*)

(PINOCCHIO *enters.*)

PINOCCHIO: Amazing, isn't it? Almost beautiful. They're like a giant graceful machine—they way they've set up camp so quickly. Just yesterday I was standing on that hill looking at a brown field. And this morning—there are tents, even a building, fences. Tell me what other nation's army could work such miracles? *(Short pause)* They're resting now. But even when they rest they can't help being active. There were a group of soldiers playing catch—their shirts off and their dog tags catching the sun. And over in another corner, I could see the Negro soldiers. I wasn't close enough to hear, but by the way they were moving, I'll bet anything they were singing. What energy those people have. It's just astonishing. *(Starts to go; stops)* He wasn't there. I'm starting to get worried. He was doing me a favor. I hope to God nothing has happened to him. I'd feel just terrible. *(He goes.)*

(CARLO stands up.)

LEONE: Who's he talking about?

MAMA: Him.

LEONE: He's looking for you?

CARLO: Forget about him. Let me finish what I was telling you. I talked to a sentry.

MAMA: And?

CARLO: And we've been declared off limits to the camp.

LEONE: Who's we?

CARLO: Us. The whole village.

MAMA: You're joking.

CARLO: I wish I was.

ROSINA: How are we supposed to eat?

LEONE: Why?

CARLO: They're worried about our black markets. That there is more than just a camp, it's supply headquarters for the whole regiment.

LEONE: That's why the meat.

MAMA: And the fish.

CARLO: And ice.

LEONE: What a pity. And I was just beginning to smell that meat.

CARLO: Maybe we can still do more than just smell it. I have an idea. We'll need your truck.

LEONE: Take it. What good is it if I can't sell it? There's no place I want to go in it.

MAMA: What's your idea?

CARLO: The sentry I know can be bribed.

ROSINA: Bribed? With what?

(PINOCCHIO *enters.*)

PINOCCHIO: I'm getting really worried now. Maybe we could organize a search. If anything's happened to that boy, it's on my conscience…. (*Sees* CARLO*)* Carlo? There you are. God, I'm happy to see you. Why didn't you tell me he was here? Did you know I was looking for you?

CARLO: No.

PINOCCHIO: I wanted to say goodbye.

CARLO: Goodbye.

(CARLO *stares at* PINOCCHIO.)

PINOCCHIO: (*Uncomfortable*) Then I'll go. (*Starts to move*) Oh, I nearly forgot—do you have my…uh….

CARLO: Your what?

PINOCCHIO: What I gave you to keep for me.

CARLO: I don't know what you're talking about. *(To the others)* Let's go.

PINOCCHIO: Carlo, my money. *(Pause)*

CARLO: What money?

(CARLO and PINOCCHIO stare at each other.)

(Long pause)

(CARLO finally turns and goes.)

PINOCCHIO: Carlo, but that isn't fair.

(End of Scene Six)

Scene Seven
AMERICAN MILLIONAIRES

(Cafe. Chairs set on the table. Late afternoon)

(PINOCCHIO, with a mop, washes the floor. SILIA, with broom, sweeps. Pause as they work)

SILIA: It's good of you to work off your bar bill like this.

PINOCCHIO: What choice do I have?

SILIA: You could have just left. Who would have stopped you?

PINOCCHIO: I always pay what I owe. You have to. If people stopped paying their debts, the world would collapse. I don't want that on my shoulders. *(Mops)*

SILIA: The world? The whole world?

PINOCCHIO: That part which is civilized, that is. If men stopped paying what they owed, the entire free enterprise system would go down the drain. And it wouldn't take much either—it's a beautiful yet fragile organism. It wouldn't take much to kill it. Just say I didn't pay back Signora Sara. Would she give credit to the next customer? I doubt it. No, it'd be cash in

advance. So without credit, the demands upon hard
currency would be so great that the value of a dollar
would be in fact greater than its purchasing power—
so prices would fall and you'd have a depression. Of
course, more money would then be printed to try to
compensate and than you'd have inflation. No, Silia,
once you stop paying your debts you are asking for
chaos, and, as chaos is the incubator of communism,
you are in fact asking for communism. So you see,
it's not out of any moral sense of responsibility that
I'm mopping this floor—I'm not getting on any high
horse doing this—I'm only doing what I consider to
be my duty—to keep the free enterprise system from
crumbling and to keep the world from the Reds.

SILIA: God!

PINOCCHIO: In America they think about things like
that. All the time. *(Mops)* It's also my hope that my
mopping here might serve as some sort of example.
I'd be lying if I said that wasn't my hope as well. This
village, I'm afraid, is nudging toward that abyss of
chaos; maybe a little of what I'm saying, and what my
actions are showing, will rub off here. I can at least
hope. What time is it?

(SILIA checks a clock.)

SILIA: Nearly five.

PINOCCHIO: Another hour and my debt will be cleared.
You know, Silia, this village—and that means all of
you—are going to have to face some tough decisions.
America's not going to bail you out forever. Sooner
or later it's going to have to come from you people.
I know it won't be easy, but the other scenario isn't
a pretty picture either. You people are on a free ride
now, but don't think it's always going to be this way.
Americans are as generous as any people in the world,
but they don't like to feel like suckers. Show them that

you're trying and they'll be there to lend a shoulder,
but try to take them for a ride and good luck. They can
be ruthless.

SILIA: You really care, don't you?

PINOCCHIO: You have to. Everyone has to. When
people stop caring, you might as well throw in the
cards. No one ever said it was going to be easy. It
takes a lot of grit and sweat and good old-fashioned
determination. That's how you turn things around.
You know, I've half a mind to stay here just to show
you people how it's done.

SILIA: How what's done?

PINOCCHIO: How to pull yourself up by your own
bootstraps. How to dream. How to make something
out of yourselves.

SILIA: But there's nothing here. There's hardly even any
food.

PINOCCHIO: So you start with nothing. It doesn't mean
you won't end up with a lot. Look at me here—I'm
making what—twenty-one cents an hour. It's a start.
And if I played my cards right, I could turn those
twenty-one cents into a million dollars inside of two
years.

SILIA: From mopping floors?

PINOCCHIO: Every American millionaire started
without much more. Mopping floors, washing dishes,
selling newspapers. Once you got your toe in the door,
all that can keep you from kicking it in is yourself.
That's what people here don't understand. It's all
"Give me, give me": I've never seen so many hands
out in my life. All of you're looking for the quick buck,
instead of looking into yourselves to find that fortune
that's out there all right, just waiting for you to pick it
up.

SILIA: But twenty-one cents an hour?

PINOCCHIO: That's where you start. The rules are so
simple every American child knows them by heart like
the pledge of allegiance. You start with twenty-one
cents, you put in twelve, fifteen, twenty hours a day—
sure, it's not easy, but who said it would be—you offer
to sleep on the floor, that way you don't pay rent and
you eat scraps and warmed-over scraps, and three-
day-old scraps, saving every penny, penny by penny,
that you can save. So you got about five dollars now
and you start to look for an investment. Something
with a high yield, nothing blue chip, it's a gamble, but
that's the name of the game—you keep your eye open
for some business that's in trouble, maybe a newsstand
and you buy in with five dollars and a lot of your
time, course you keep mopping floors, so now you're
working maybe twenty-two hours a day, but you
take the night shift so you can sleep without anybody
knowing that you're sleeping; so you're putting
more and more dollars into the newsstand, and by
sheer stamina you are wearing your partner down—
preferably he's an old man without much ambition
left in him, and without any sons—so you become
like a son to him so he trusts you, and so he doesn't
question when you split your interest in the newsstand
and sell half for twenty bucks which you immediately
invest in a share of a shoe store; course, you collect the
twenty fast and drag your feet on paying the twenty
to the shoe store owner, because during that delay you
can loan the twenty out at short term to some widow
or family with a sick mother who needs the cash fast
and are willing to pay good interest—and you make
them pay up when the shoe store owner threatens to
go to court; so now you own a part of a shoe store, a
part of a newsstand and you got a reputation in the
neighborhood for short-term loans. Now of course

you're still mopping floors so the next five dollars you save you open another newsstand across the street from the one you partially own and try to drive the old man and your other partner out of business. You take a bath for a month by undercutting their prices—you're selling the Tribune now for one cent and giving away free coffee. The old man who's like a father to you can't hold his own now, his customers are now your customers and they may be looking sheepish when they buy from you but who can pass up that free cup of coffee? So you make an offer to buy full control of the old man's newsstand—for five bucks—on credit—he sells and so you burn it down to collect the insurance— fifty bucks you get because you went to the biggest insurance company you could find and it wasn't worth their bother to investigate. So you got forty-five dollars now in cash—you paid the old man the five—see, that's what I was telling you about always paying what you owed—and a newsstand that sells coffee for a dime and the Trib for four cents and part of a shoe store and you're still mopping floors.

So you follow a similar scenario with the shoe store but instead of burning it down you open a new shop as a discount store, which means you just raise the prices in the other store and you call yourself a chain. You start giving credit called "lay-a-way plan", which means they pay some now and the rest later, but if they don't pay the rest later, you keep the money they've already put down. If they don't like it, let them sue. This inability to pay is highly likely if you've picked the right neighborhood. So what you have is a pure profit, which of course you invest in short-term loans. Now, should they come up with the rest of the payment, you stall them on delivering their goods because you haven't yet purchased their goods yourself or if you have you've sold them already.

So you're still mopping floors—but not for much
longer—and you've got a newsstand empire and a
chain of shoe stores and a loan business on the side
where you charge nine-point-nine percent—ten
percent is against the law in American, ten percent is
considered usury. But the road is not as smooth as you
might think. Health inspectors are starting to look into
the stands where you are also selling hot dogs now,
and fire marshals are on your back because all your
back exits in your shoe shops have been covered by
inventory—space after all is at a premium. So here's
one of the big hurdles you are going to have to face—
in America there are so many god damn regulations,
I don't know how the government expects a man to
make an honest buck. I wish it would just get off our
backs, but it won't so you finally realize you need
political connections. But you are still a small fry—
so what can you do for them? Except maybe give
them a free meal every now and then. So one day
you throw down your mop and walk into the office
of the restaurant owner and toss an envelope full of
greenbacks on his desk and buy him out.
That's the last mopping you do—if you've gotten
married to a nice girl who believes in you and stands
beside you, you give her the mop, as you know what
twenty-onc cents an hour can mount to and you don't
want some smart-ass kid in there breathing down
your neck. So you've stopped mopping, and you've
diversified your investments, so your collateral is
top drawer, but you still have only fifty bucks in
hard cash in your pocket; so one day you walk into
Chase Manhattan Bank and take out a loan for twenty
thousand dollars and start to play with the big boys in
the open market—while keeping up the insurance just
to hedge your bet, and you open an office on Madison
Avenue, hire an English secretary and change your

name to Robert Buckingham. And there you have it—
an American millionaire in the making!

(Pause)

SILIA: But you only have twenty thousand, how do you
make the rest?

PINOCCHIO: With an office on Madison Avenue,
with an English secretary and a name like Robert
Buckingham, you can't fail to become a millionaire in
America.

(Long pause. PINOCCHIO and SILIA work.)

SILIA: And the wife? She's still mopping the floor at the
restaurant?

PINOCCHIO: He probably divorced her.

SILIA: Oh, God, why? I liked her.

PINOCCHIO: She got fat. American millionaires like
skinny women. With high cheek-bones.

(Pause)

SILIA: Oh.

(PINOCCHIO and SILIA work.)

SILIA: But how could he divorce her, isn't he Catholic?

PINOCCHIO: He bought a new stained glass window for
a seminary in Westchester County.

(Noise of the truck off. SILIA looks out the window.)

SILIA: It's Carlo and Father. Where can they be going?

(End of Scene Seven)

Scene Eight
THE CRIME

(LEONE's *newspaper office. Table. Three chairs.* LEONE *and* CARLO *at the table. Beef on the table.*)

(*Evening*)

(*Pause*)

CARLO: Should I serve?

LEONE: Wait for Mama.

(*Short pause.* CARLO *sniffs.*)

CARLO: Smell.

(LEONE *sniffs.* CARLO *runs his finger across the beef and licks his finger.*)

CARLO: Here, let me give you a taste. While we're waiting for Mama.

LEONE: While we're waiting.

(CARLO *cuts a small piece, gives it to* LEONE, *who eats;* LEONE *groans with pleasure.*)

LEONE: Here. Let me give you a slice.

(*Cuts a slice, gives it to* CARLO, *who eats and groans.*)

LEONE: American.

CARLO: How can you tell?

LEONE: Process of elimination. Who else has beef? Mushroom?

(CARLO *takes a mushroom.* LEONE *takes a few.*)

CARLO: How many are you taking?

LEONE: I took two. Here, take another so we'll be even.

CARLO: You took three.

LEONE: One was just the stem. Easy on the sauce.

CARLO: Maybe I should carve. Unless, of course, you...?

LEONE: No. No. Carve. *(Short pause)* By all means carve.

(CARLO carves.)

CARLO: Your plate.

(LEONE hands him his plate; CARLO serves.)

(Pause)

(Suddenly CARLO and LEONE look at each other and start laughing—they laugh to the point of hysterics—then start eating, shoveling the food in, groaning. They eat like they've been starving.)

MAMA: *(Entering with a plate)* The potatoes are done. You didn't wait for me!

LEONE: *(With his mouth full)* It was getting cold.

MAMA: It wasn't getting cold. I said, it wasn't getting cold.

LEONE: I don't have time to talk to you now.

(MAMA digs in and eats like the other two.)

CARLO: Where's the butter?

LEONE: Didn't you get the butter?

CARLO: I wasn't supposed to get the butter.

LEONE: I got the mushrooms.

(They eat.)

MAMA: *(With her mouth full)* Where's your mother?

CARLO: She said she wanted to eat alone so she could enjoy it more.

LEONE: I can understand that.

MAMA: *(To CARLO)* Slow down. That's your third piece.

(They eat.)

(Bell off. After a pause, PINOCCHIO *enters. No one notices; he watches them.)*

PINOCCHIO: *(Finally:)* Where did all that come from?

(They look up but keep eating.)

PINOCCHIO: I thought the American camp was off limits.

(They ignore PINOCCHIO.*)*

PINOCCHIO: Carlo, do you have anything for me?

CARLO: Only enough for the three of us.

PINOCCHIO: That's not what I'm talking about. And you know it.

(Pause. They eat.)

PINOCCHIO: How could you do it, Carlo? You think you can just steal and get away with it? *(Pause)* You think the world owes you something, Carlo? You've got a big shock ahead of you, if you think that.

LEONE: What do you what? Can't you see we're eating?

PINOCCHIO: I came to say goodbye.

MAMA: *(With mouth full)* He's leaving.

PINOCCHIO: Tonight.

(Pause)

LEONE: I'd shake your hand, but mine's greasy.

(They eat.)

*(*PINOCCHIO *leaves.)*

CARLO: How could you have forgotten the butter? It's a crime.

(End of Scene Eight)

Scene Nine
THE BLOOD OF SAINT CATHERINE

(ROSINA's cart. Morning. Bright sun. She sits and leans against her cart, her eyes closed. LEONE enters, he walks slowly. After a while he looks at her.)

LEONE: Sleep well?

ROSINA: I slept content. (Wipes the air in front of her face.) Gnats. They smell my breath. (Giggles)

LEONE: You know how I slept?

ROSINA: Just tell me.

LEONE: Like an American. Ever seen an American sleep?

ROSINA: Don't get personal.

LEONE: They sleep with little smiles across their faces. And they don't have nightmares.

ROSINA: No?

LEONE: Only dreams.

ROSINA: So what did you dream about?

LEONE: I was on the side of a hill. And I was plowing. Suddenly my mule—I had a mule—it broke away from me. I tried to chase it, but the lightning made it run fast. It started to rain cats and dogs. The field was all mud, and I was up to my knees in it. I tried to pull at my boots but slipped, and that's when I found out….

ROSINA: Found out what?

LEONE: That the mud was chocolate. Swiss chocolate.

ROSINA: So you kept eating right through your sleep.

LEONE: The whole time. I can still taste that chocolate.

ROSINA: And the rain, was it wine?

LEONE: No. No. Just rain.

ROSINA: Too bad. And Mama?

LEONE: She wasn't in my dream.

ROSINA: Did she sleep well?

LEONE: She slept at the table. With her head on a plate. If I'd had an apple, I would have put it in her mouth. *(Laughs)* Where's Carlo, we were going to go back to the camp this morning.

ROSINA: He's probably still in bed, dreaming of chocolate like you.

LEONE: Is that how you left him?

ROSINA: *(Shrugs)* I slept out here last night. And I watched the stars.

LEONE: And the moon that looks like cheese.

(A woman's scream in the distance. LEONE and ROSINA look at each other.)

WIFE: *(From the first scene. Off)* Hurry! Hurry! Come!

ROSINA: *(To LEONE)* What is it?

LEONE: I don't know.

WIFE: *(Running in)* Hurry. Come quick. Go look! Look!

LEONE: Look at what?

(LEONE grabs WIFE, she is crying.)

WIFE: Get a priest! *(She falls on her knees.)*

(Church bells begin to toll.)

LEONE: What's going on?

(LEONE runs off. WIFE on her knees prays in Latin.)

ROSINA: You, watch my cart.

(ROSINA starts to run off, MAMA hurries in.)

MAMA: *(To WIFE:)* What is it, an air raid?

ROSINA: Ask her. I don't know. *(She runs out.)*

MAMA: What did you see? Quit that and tell me, what did you see?

WIFE: Get a priest. Hurry! It's happened! *(Continues to pray, bell continues to toll.)*

MAMA: *(More to herself)* What's happened? *(Looks up at the sky)* I don't hear any planes.

WIFE: Get a priest and pray. It's a miracle.

MAMA: What's a miracle? Where's everyone running to? What did you see?!

WIFE: A miracle!

LEONE: *(Running in)* It's a miracle!

MAMA: What is? Where? *(Stopping him)*

LEONE: The fountain. Where's Silia? She should see this. She wasn't old enough before, but now she is.

MAMA: Leone, what are you talking about? What is happening?!

LEONE: Go look at the fountain. Go!

MAMA: What is it?

LEONE: The water's turned to blood!

MAMA: Oh, my God. Saint Catherine's blood?

LEONE: Of course!

MAMA: It's a miracle? Where's Silia, she should see this. *(She runs out.)*

WIFE: Get a priest!

LEONE: *(To WIFE:)* Who knows about this? Do the Americans know? They'll kill just to pay to see this. We should put up a fence. So we can control the crowds. Where's Carlo? Carlo!!!

ROSINA: *(Hurries in)* And you said there'd be no more miracles.

LEONE: When did I say that?

ROSINA: You and everybody else. How dare you call yourselves Catholics. Look. *(Shows her hand, which has blood on it)*

LEONE: You touched it?

ROSINA: Of course I touched it. I have arthritis, don't I? *(She goes to her cart.)*

LEONE: Don't you think we should put up a fence?

ROSINA: What do we need a fence for?

LEONE: To make sure everyone pays.

ROSINA: I'll have Carlo help you.

LEONE: What are you doing?

ROSINA: *(Taking bottles from the cart)* If it can cure arthritis, who knows what drinking it can do. *(She starts to run off.)*

LEONE: Wait. Do you have any more bottles?

ROSINA: Find your own. *(She runs off.)*

LEONE: My wife has some bottles. *(Starts to go)*

MAMA: *(Entering)* Leone, where are you going?

LEONE: Go get some bottles.

MAMA: What for?

LEONE: Do you know how much that blood is worth?

(MAMA starts to run off.)

WIFE: Did they get a priest?

MAMA: *(Over her shoulder while she's running)* One's coming. *(She leaves.)*

LEONE: Wait. Were you the first to see it?

WIFE: I don't know.

LEONE: Did you see it turn from water to blood?

WIFE: I don't know. It was blood when I walked by.

LEONE: Did you hear any voices?

WIFE: Voices?

LEONE: Sometimes with a miracle you also hear voices.

WIFE: I don't know. Maybe.

LEONE: You know, they could make you a saint for this.

WIFE: A saint? Oh, God. Where's the priest? *(She hurries off toward the fountain.)*

MAMA: This is all I could carry, there's more in the shed.

LEONE: Did you find Silia?

MAMA: She wasn't home.

LEONE: Then she's going to miss it.

MAMA: Maybe it'll last.

LEONE: The first miracle since before the war, don't hold your breath.

MAMA: *(Looking off)* What's she doing?

LEONE: She jumped in. She wants to be a saint.

MAMA: She could defile the blood. Stop her!

ROSINA: *(Enters with filled bottles)* That woman's going to ruin it for all of us. Who's going to want to drink blood that she's been swimming in.

LEONE: How much did you get?

ROSINA: A couple of liters. But I'm running low on bottles. How much do you want for your tub?

MAMA: It's not for sale.

(WIFE suddenly lets out a piercing scream, off.)

(Pause)

(The bells continue.)

ROSINA: What happened?

LEONE: Oh, Christ. *(He runs to the fountain.)*

ROSINA: What is it, I can't see?

MAMA: It's a body.

ROSINA: A body? Another miracle? A body rising from the blood of Saint Catherine. Dear God. *(Crosses herself)* Let's go see.

(They move.)

MAMA: Wait.

ROSINA: *(Pulling at MAMA)* Let's get closer.

(LEONE hurries in.)

LEONE: *(To MAMA)* Hold her back.

(MAMA grabs ROSINA.)

ROSINA: Let me go. Why can't I see? What is it? *(Fighting now)* What is it?

LEONE: It's Carlo.

ROSINA: Carlo?

ROSINA: It's his blood. His throat was cut from ear to ear.

ROSINA: Let me go!!!!!

LEONE: Where's Silia? I don't want her to see this.

MAMA: *(Fighting)*, Get a priest! Get a priest!

(Bells continue.)

(End of Scene Nine)

Scene Ten
DISTANT BELLS

(Field near train tracks—same as Scene One. The church bells in the distance. LUCIO [of Scene One] leans against a stick and smokes.)

(Pause)

(Suddenly a woman's groan off. LUCIO flinches, smokes. A train whistle in the distance.)

(SILIA enters. She is trembling, white.)

SILIA: It's coming. I hear it.

(LUCIO nods.)

SILIA: Does it usually slow down?

LUCIO: Sometimes. Sometimes it doesn't.

SILIA: I'll take my chances.

(Train getting closer)

SILIA: Here. Thank you.

(SILIA hands LUCIO the wire she's been holding.)

SILIA: It's in the ditch. Could you bury it?

(Without looking at SILIA, LUCIO nods.)

SILIA: I wonder what the bells are for? *(Short pause)* Goodbye. Tell my parents, will you? It won't be hard.

(Train closer)

SILIA: I better go to the tracks. *(She looks back.)*

LUCIO: Silia?

SILIA: Yes?

LUCIO: Why?

SILIA: Because American millionaires like their women skinny.

(Train loud)

(SILIA *runs.*)

SILIA: Slow down! Slow down! *(She's off.)*

(Train noise very loud)

(End of Scene Ten)

Scene Eleven
WEEKS LATER

(On a train. PINOCCHIO *and an American* SOLDIER *in uniform, who reads a book.)*

PINOCCHIO: What are you reading?

SOLDIER: What?

PINOCCHIO: I asked what you're reading.

SOLDIER: A book.

*(*PINOCCHIO *makes a face.)*

PINOCCHIO: I know that, what kind of book. A mystery?

SOLDIER: Yes. A mystery. *(Goes back to his reading)*

PINOCCHIO: I thought so. You Americans are always reading mysteries. Is there a private eye?

SOLDIER: A what?

PINOCCHIO: Is there a private eye? In the mystery?

SOLDIER: I haven't gotten to the murder yet, so how should I know if there's a private eye?

(Pause)

PINOCCHIO: It usually says on the back if there is.

SOLDIER: *(Looks at him)* I didn't read the back. *(Reads)*

PINOCCHIO: Oh. *(Short pause)* Do you mind if I read the back?

SOLDIER: Yes.

PINOCCHIO: Oh. *(Pause)* Are you a real American?

SOLDIER: Look, buster, what do you want to say?

PINOCCHIO: I only ask because Americans are usually so open. You ask them a question and they spill out their whole lives. Americans wear their hearts on their sleeves.

SOLDIER: I'm an American. *(Reads)*

PINOCCHIO: Ever been to Italy?

SOLDIER: North Africa.

PINOCCHIO: I was just in Italy. Actually, I come from Italy. So it was sort of like going home. My father's dead. But it's a small village so I had lots of people to see. Italians love Americans. They look to America. I couldn't tell them enough about America. Their curiosity was inexhaustible. That's nice to see. I mean, because you hear so many stories. How they hate Americans. And some of that's there all right. Course, they all think we're millionaires. They got a lot of fantasies like that about America. They may love us, but they sure don't understand us. And that's why they're always trying to take advantage. What they don't realize is that we may be very open people, you understand, that we really want to be good and do good and all that, but it doesn't mean we're pushovers. It's like with a child, you spoil them and they'll end up rotten. You got to be tough with them—it's for their own good. They got to stand on their own two feet sometime, so they better start learning soon. Don't you think? *(Short pause)* I mean, America can't do everything. Even if we could, they'd still just end up resenting us. You know what I think?

SOLDIER: Tell me.

PINOCCHIO: I think that the best thing we can give those people—and those people are my people, or

they once were my people, because that's where my
roots are and roots are important, we often forget that
because we're such a mobile population, but they are
important and that's why it's important to keep those
ties, even if it's just writing back and telling the folks
how well you're doing—they take pride in that, it
gives them something to talk about. But anyway, I was
saying what we should give these people—it's not food
or clothes or new technologies, that's not what they
really need—what they need is an American spirit. We
got to teach them what we know almost instinctively
from birth, and that's that if you want to do something,
you can. It's all up to you. The only thing that's
standing in your way is yourself. That's what they
got to learn. And that's something positive. And
that's why the Reds don't have an iceberg's chance in
hell against us Americans. Because we are teaching
something positive, and everything they're teaching
is negative. We tell people to hope and they're telling
people to give up. They are telling people to quit, and
people—in my experience—don't like quitters. No.
And they never will. *(Short pause)* We're a super power
now; we got the bomb, we can do whatever we want
in the world. We can take over the whole world if we
wanted to. But we don't want to—and that says about
all that needs to be said about America. All we want is
for people to be free. Like us. So we get kicked in the
teeth sometimes. That's sometimes the cost of trying
to help people. But that's not going to make us run
away from our responsibilities. Everybody's looking
toward America. The eyes of the world are upon us.
Everybody's asking themselves—what kind of people
are these new giants? That's why we got to show
them we won't take any shit, and once they see that,
the better off we'll all be. *(Short pause)* We're slowing
down. *(Short pause)* Can you read the station sign?

SOLDIER: Iowa City.

PINOCCHIO: Iowa City. Look at those fields. This country is so big. It takes your breath away. A man can do as he wants here. *(Pause)* How's the book?

SOLDIER: It's getting better. *(Short pause)* I got to the murder.

(Pause)

END OF PLAY

www.ingramcontent.com/pod-product-compliance
Lightning Source LLC
Chambersburg PA
CBHW070032110426
42741CB00035B/2734